Fun Facts about Oxygen Chemistry for Kids

The Element Series

Children's Chemistry Books

Speedy Publishing LLC
40 E. Main St. #1156
Newark, DE 19711
www.speedypublishing.com

Oxygen is one of the most important elements as it is needed by most forms of live to survive on Earth. You may think of it as the air we breathe. It is known as the third most abundant element in our universe and the most abundant in your body. Read further to learn more about this element such as its characteristics, its uses, and how it was discovered.

Characteristics and Properties of Oxygen

Oxygen consists of 8 protons and 8 electrons. It can found at the top of column 16 of the periodic table.

8

O

Oxygen

15.9994

Water Molecules H2O

Under usual conditions it forms a gas composed of molecules made of two oxygen atoms (O2). This is known as a diatomic gas. It its gaseous form it is odorless, colorless, and tasteless. Additionally, it exists as O3, the allotrope ozone. The ozone exists in an upper region of the atmosphere of the Earth, creating an ozone layer which protects us from the sun's harmful rays.

Even though we have this ozone layer, we should still wear sunscreen every day. In its pure state, it is very reactive and it can create compounds from several other elements. It dissolves in water quickly.

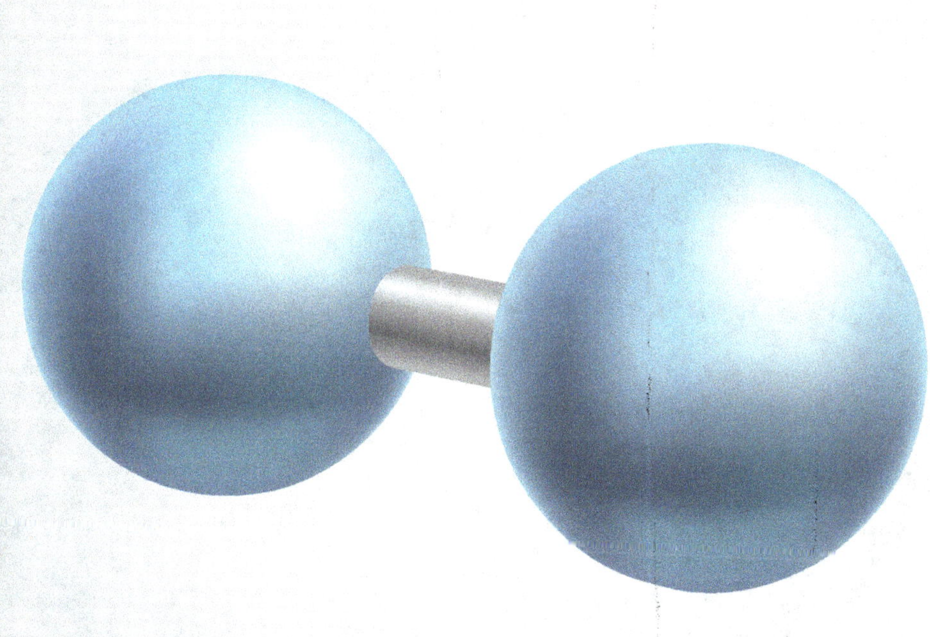

O₂

Oxygen

H2O molecule

Oxidation is the process of combining it with different atoms to make compounds.

Electrolysis is the process of converting water to hydrogen and oxygen.

When concentrated, it promotes a quick combustion. This is why you see "No Smoking" signs around people that are using it for breathing.

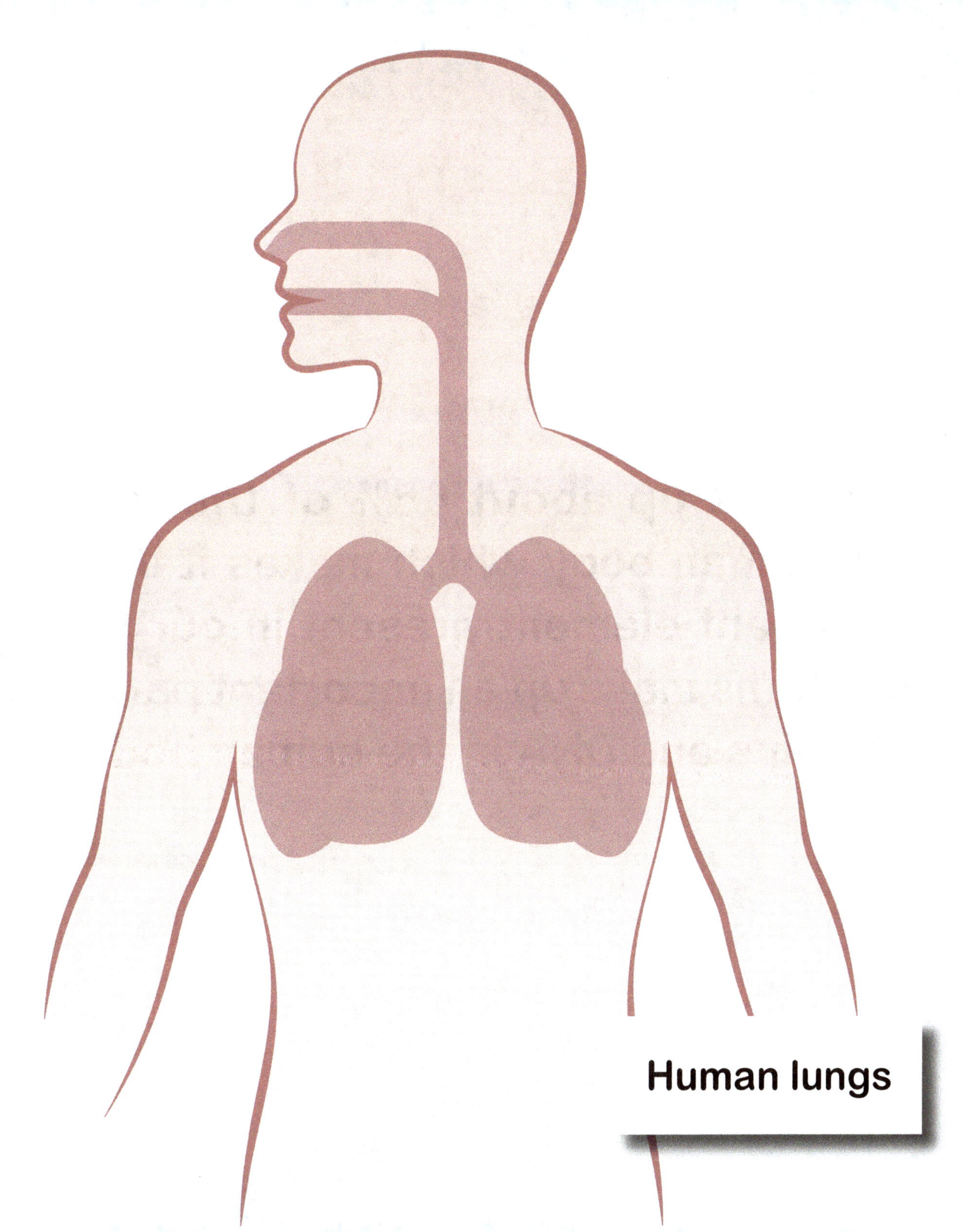
Human lungs

It makes up about 65% of the mass of the human body which makes it the most abundant element present in our bodies. Its atoms make up an important part of the proteins and DNA in the human body.

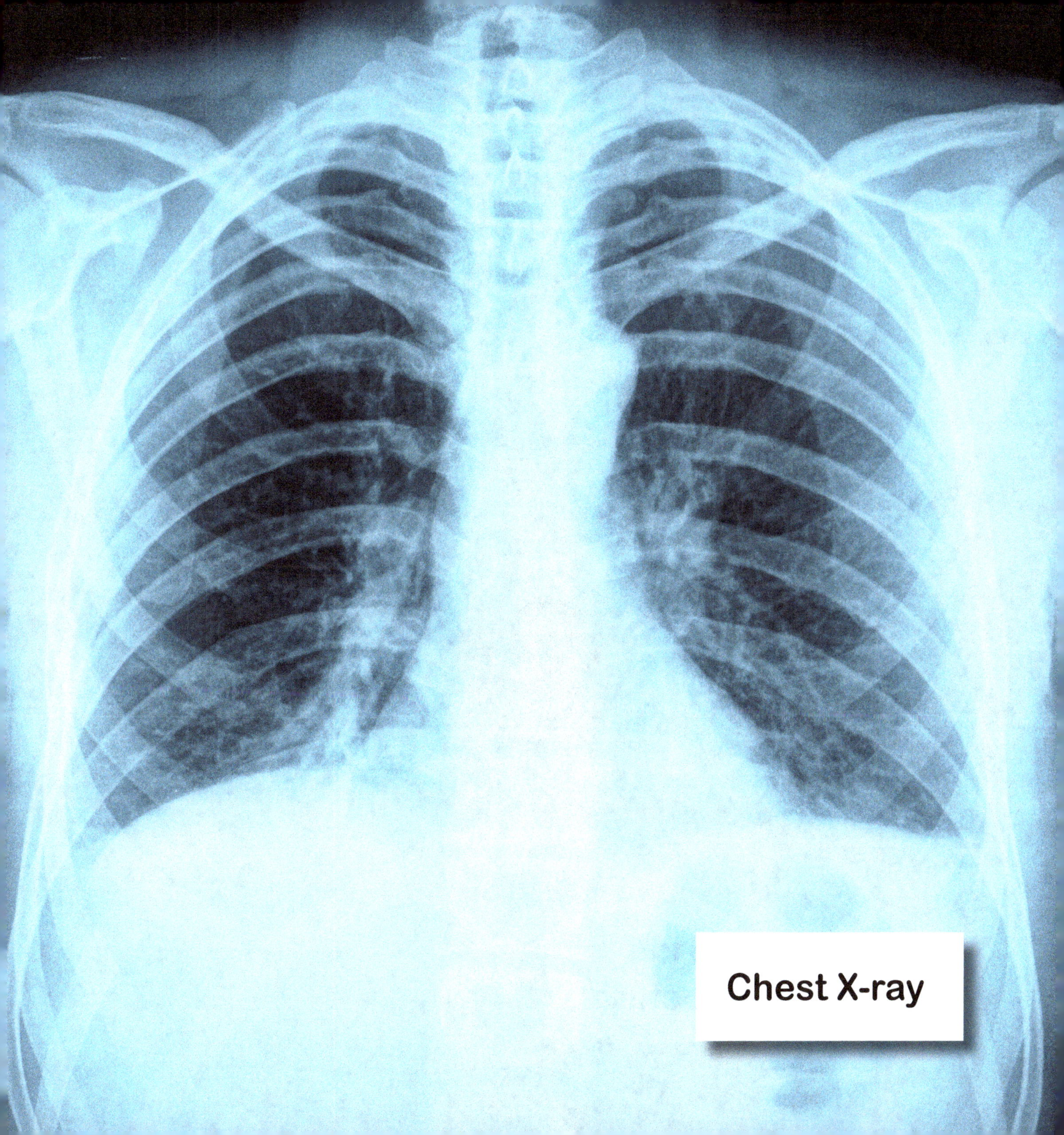
Chest X-ray

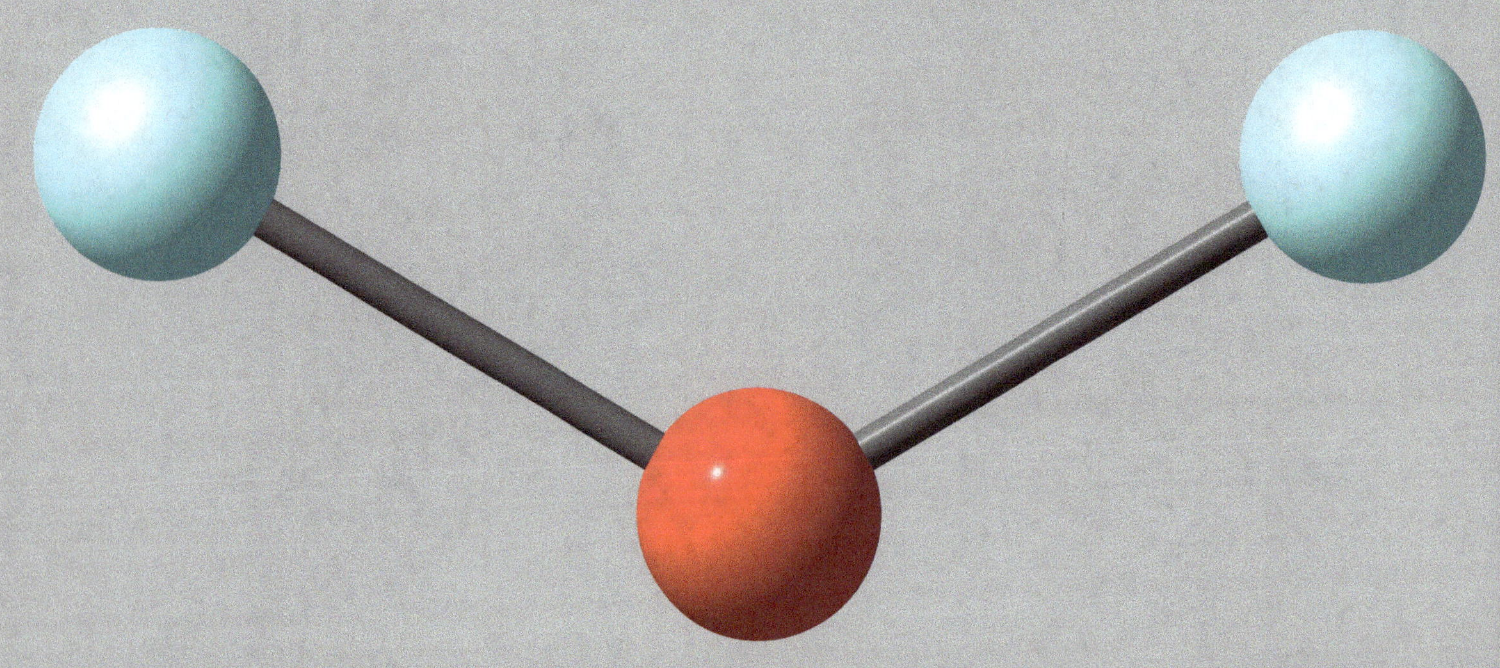

Oxygen difluoride
molecular structure

Oxygen Forms

Dioxygen is the common allotrope of its elemental form on Earth, O2. It is most commonly found in this form, including approximately 21% of the atmosphere of the Earth. Its bond length is 121 pm and has an energy bond of 48 kJ/mol. Oxygen is a colorless gas and has a boils at -183 degrees Celsius.

Singlet oxygen is the name used in the diamagnetic form of O2. Due to the unusual properties, it can persist for longer than an hour at room temperature, dependent upon its environment. Due to the difference of its electron shells, the chemical properties of singlet and triplet oxygen can vary. Singlet oxygen is what can damage sunlight on organic materials such as polymers.

Oxygen

View of the earth from space

Ozone is a triatomic molecule and contains three oxygen atoms. As an allotrope, it is much less stable that its diatomic allotrope. It is a pollutant in the air and can cause respiratory difficulties. However, it is beneficial in the upper layer of the atmosphere and can prevent damaging ultraviolet light reaching the surface of the Earth. There are many ways it can be used in consumer and industrial applications.

Tetraoxygen is suspected to have existed since early 1900s, then known as oxozone. It was then identified in 2001 at the University of Rome by a team organized by F. Cacace. O_4 is a molecule thought to be a solid phase which later was identified as O_8. This team felt that O_4 more than likely consisted of two O_2 molecules that looked similar to dumbbells, and held loosely together by forces induced by dipole dispersion.

Ozone Molecule Ball
And Stick Model

Liquid water
hydrogen bonds

Solid Oxygen consists of 6 distinct phases. One appears as a cluster of dark-red O_8. When it is exposed to 96 GPa pressure, it appears metallic, similar to hydrogen, it then becomes heavier such as chalcogens, similar to polonium and tellurium, both that show a substantial metallic character. When it occurs in temperatures that are very low, it also becomes a superconductor.

Liquid oxygen is also known as LOX, or Lox in the gas, submarine, and aerospace industries. It is light blue in color and strongly paramagnetic and can suspend among poles of a powerful horseshoe magnet. Its density is 1.141 g/cm3 and its freezing point is 50.5K which makes is a cryogenic. It is classified as an industrial gas and widely used for medical and industrial purposes. It is obtained from the oxygen naturally found in the air by fractional distillation. It has a ratio expansion of 861.1 when at 68 degrees Fahrenheit (20 degrees Celsius and is used as breathing oxygen in military and commercial aircraft.

OXIDIZING GAS 2
OXYGEN
UN 1072
NET WEIGHT
20 KG
FOR INDUSTRIAL USE ONLY
OXIDIZING GAS 2
OXYGEN
UN 1072
NET WEIGHT
25 KG
FOR INDUSTRIAL USE ONLY
OXIDIZING GAS 2
OXYGEN
UN 1072
NET WEIGHT
10 KG
FOR INDUSTRIAL USE ONLY
OXIDIZING GAS 2
OXYGEN
UN 1072
NET WEIGHT
8 KG
OXIDIZING GAS 2
OXYGEN
UN 1072
NET WEIGHT
6 KG

Where can it be found on Earth?

It is all around us. It is considered to be one of the most significant element on this planet. Earth is the only planet in our solar system that contains a high percentage of it. Approximately 21% of our atmosphere and 50% of the Earth's crust mass is made up of it. Water is made using one atom of it (H_2O). It is also considered a substantial element of life on this planet.

The Oxygen Cycle

This cycle is a biogeochemical and describes how it moves between its main three reservoirs, including the atmosphere, the content of biological matter in our biosphere, which is the global sum of all of the ecosystems, and lithosphere, the Earth's crust.

The Oxygen Cycle

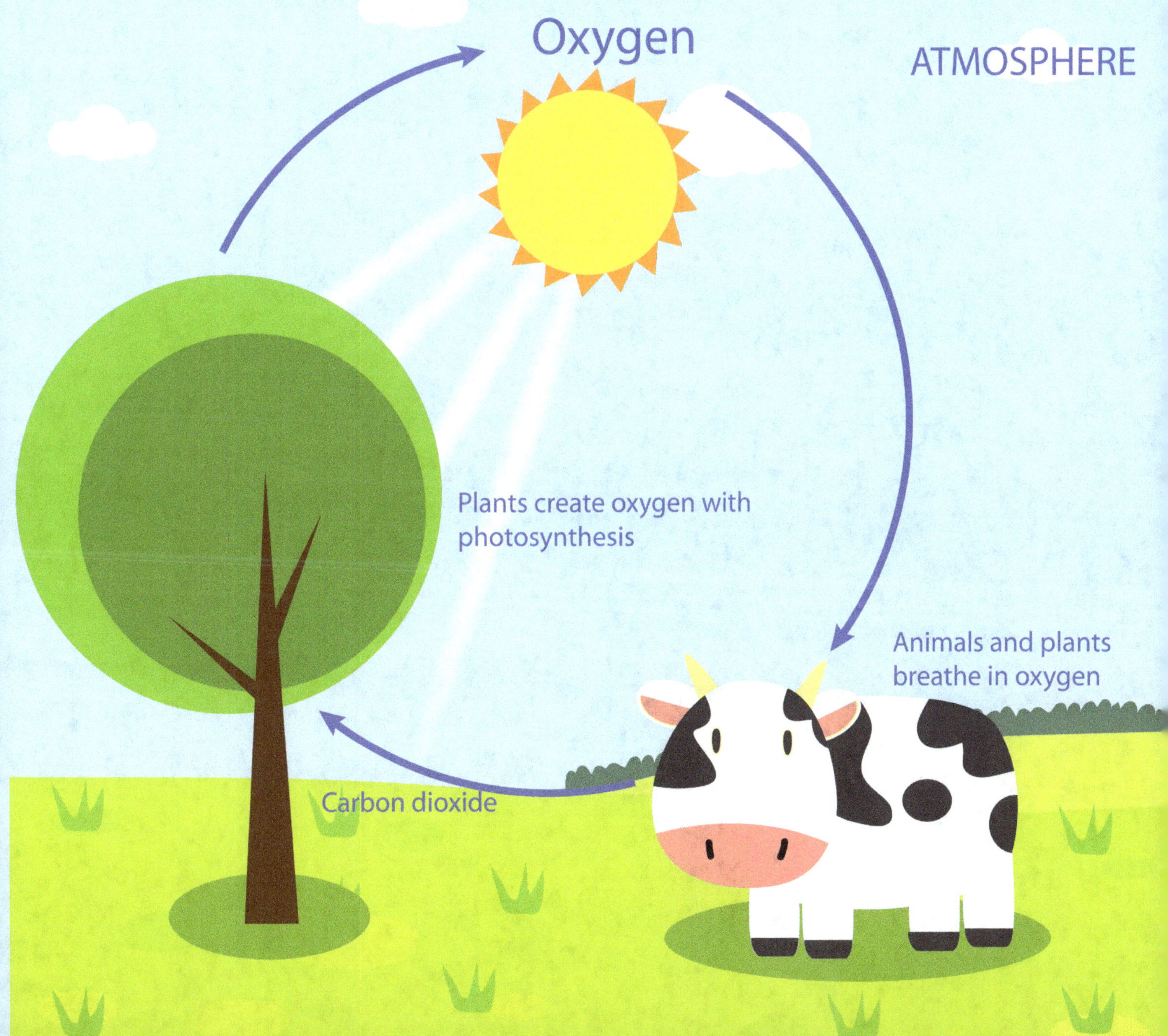

Failures in this cycle can result in development of hypoxic zones. The main factor of this cycle is photosynthesis, which results in our atmosphere and life.

How do we use it today?

It is used by plants and animals in their breathing (respiration) process. Photosynthesis produces the oxygen found in our atmosphere. There would be only a small amount of it in the air without plants.

Two oxygen cylinders

Have you seen tanks filled with oxygen? These are used in the medical field for people that have difficulty breathing. They are also used by scuba divers and astronauts for breathing.

In industry, it is used for steel manufacturing. It is also used to make new compounds similar to plastics and generating a hot flame as is used in welding. Rocket Fuel is made when liquid oxygen is mixed with liquid hydrogen.

REFILL
1000 2000
3000 PSI
OXYGEN
USE NO OIL
MADE IN U.S.A.

How was it discovered?

One of the first experiments regarding the reaction between air and combustion was done by Philo of Byzantium, a 2nd century Greek writer. In Pneumatica, Philo detected when inverting a container over a candle that is burning and surrounding it with water would result in some of the water rising. He incorrectly deduced that some of the air was converted into fire and had the ability to escape amid the pores of the glass. Centuries later Leonardo da Vinci expanded on Philo's work by noting that a portion of it is consumed throughout respiration and combustion.

In 1772, it was first discovered by a Swedish chemist named C. W. Steele. He referred to this gas as "fire air" since it was required to burn fire. He did not issue his findings immediately and the element was then discovered in 1774 by Joseph Priestley.

Medical Oxygen
Concentrator

Scuba diving tanks

Its name stems from the Greek word "oxygenes" meaning "acid producer". Early chemists thought it was used for all acids. It was named this since early chemists felt that it was required for all acids.

Isotopes

Isotopes consist of variants of an element that differ in their number of neutrons.

8
O
Oxygen
15.9994

oxygen

8

Each isotope of a particular element contains equal proton numbers in each of their atoms. Isotope stems from the Greek term isos (equal) combined with topos (place), which means same place. Hence, the meaning different isotopes of a particular element reside on the periodic table in the same position.

Oxygen consists of three stable isotopes, O-16, O-17, and O-18. Its relative atomic mass is 15.9994(3). More than 99% of stable oxygen consists of isotope oxygen-16. Its isotopes are known to range in their mass from 12 to 24.

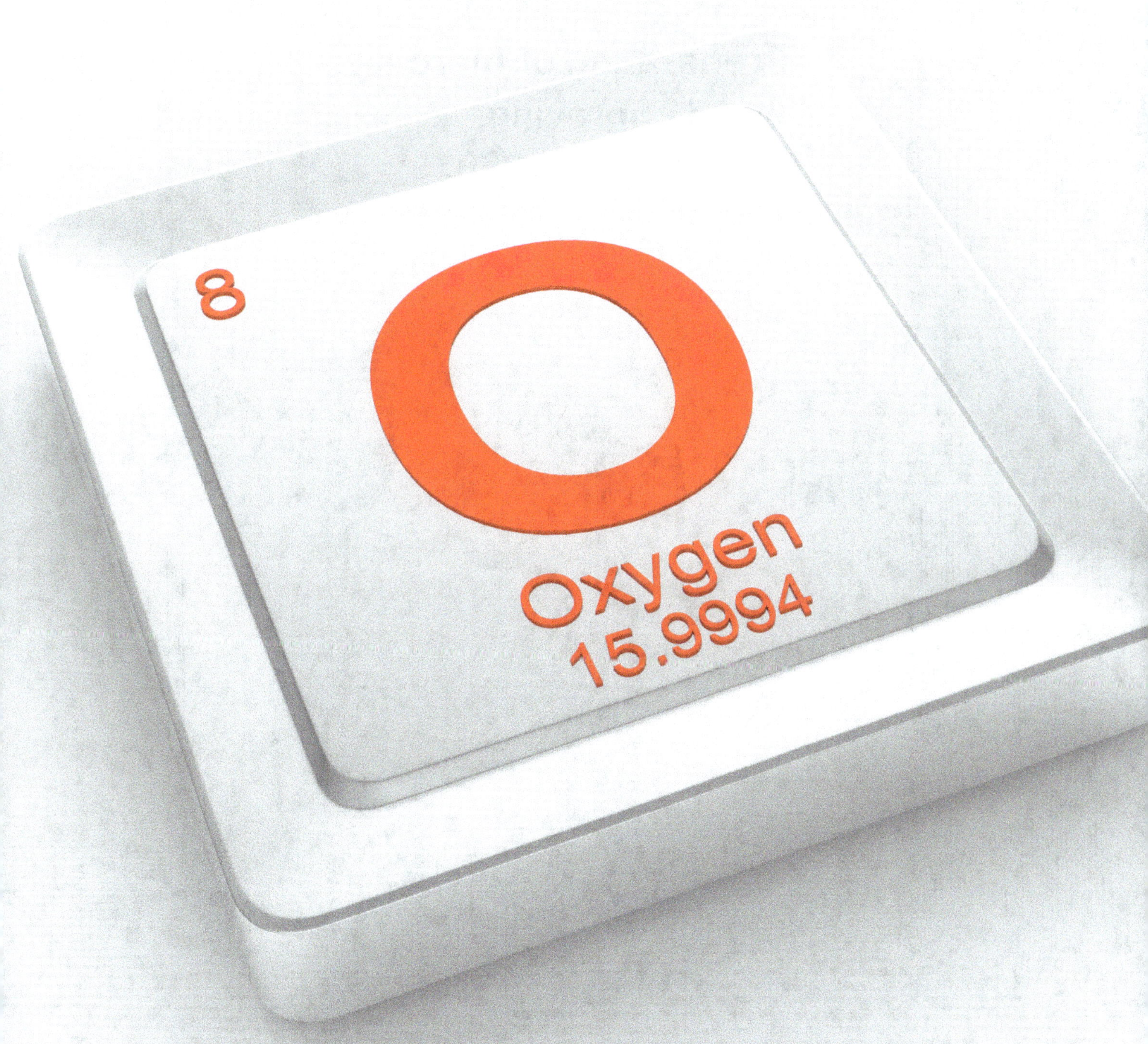
8
O
Oxygen
15.9994

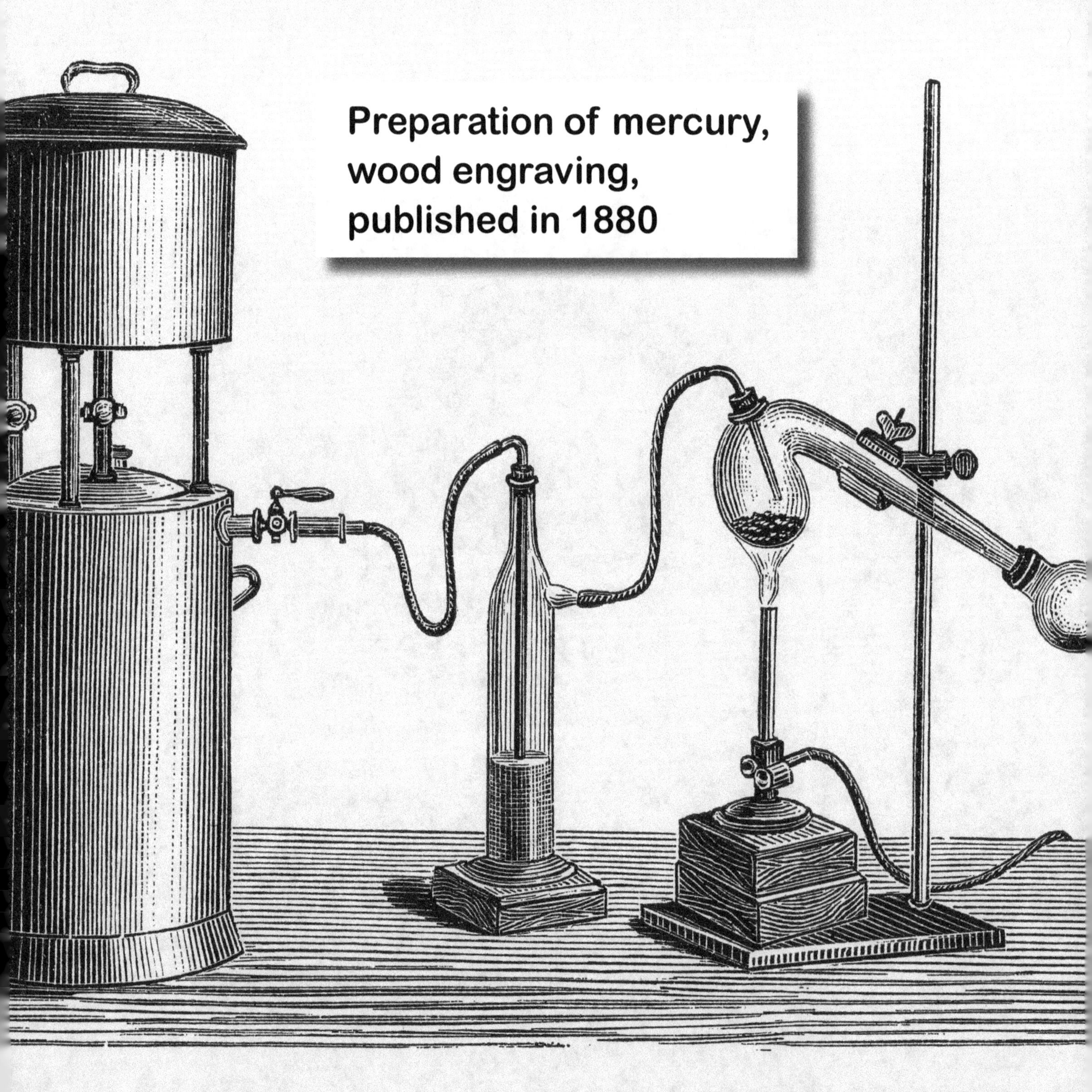

Preparation of mercury,
wood engraving,
published in 1880

Toxicity

Oxygen toxicity results when we breathe molecular oxygen at partial elevated pressures. It is also referred to as oxygen intoxication, oxygen poisoning, and toxicity syndrome. The central nervous system toxicity was known as the Paul Bert effect and the pulmonary condition was known as the Lorrain Smith effect. More severe toxicity can result in damage to cells, and even death, with the central nervous system and eyes being most affected. It is also a major issue with scuba divers, people using a high concentration, in particular, premature babies, the people using hyperbaric oxygen therapy.

Periodic Table of Elements

There is so much more to learn about this element as well as the many other elements. You may want to research the periodic table of elements which lists all the elements including their atomic structure. In 1869, a Russian chemist named Dmitri Mendeleev came up with this table. With the use of this table, he had the ability to predict properties of elements prior to them being discovered.

PERIODIC TABLE OF THE ELEMENTS

Atomic weight — 1.008 — Atomic number — 1
Symbol — H
Name — Hydrogen

1.008 1 H Hydrogen																	4,0026 2 He Helium
6.941 3 Li Lithium	9.012 4 Be Beryllium											10,811 5 B Boron	12,011 6 C Carbon	14,007 7 N Nitrogen	15,999 8 O Oxygen	18,998 9 F Fluorine	20,179 10 Ne Neon
22.99 11 Na Sodium	24.31 12 Mg Magnesium											26.98 13 Al Aluminium	28,086 14 Si Silicon	30.97 15 P Phosphorus	32,066 16 S Sulfur	35,452 17 Cl Chlorine	39,948 18 Ar Argon
39.10 19 K Potassium	40.08 20 Ca Calcium	44.96 21 Sc Scandium	47.87 22 Ti Titanium	50.94 23 V Vanadium	52.00 24 Cr Chromium	54.94 25 Mn Manganese	55.85 26 Fe Iron	58.93 27 Co Cobalt	58.69 28 Ni Nickel	63.55 29 Cu Copper	65.38 30 Zn Zinc	69.72 31 Ga Gallium	72.63 32 Ge Germanium	74.92 33 As Arsenic	78.96 34 Se Selenium	79,904 35 Br Bromine	83,80 36 Kr Krypton
85.47 37 Rb Rubidium	87.62 38 Sr Strontium	88.91 39 Y Yttrium	91.22 40 Zr Zirconium	95.96 41 Nb Niobium	92.91 42 Mo Molybdenum	97,907 43 Tc Technetium	101.1 44 Ru Ruthenium	102.9 45 Rh Rhodium	106.4 46 Pd Palladium	107.9 47 Ag Silver	112.4 48 Cd Cadmium	114.8 49 In Indium	118.7 50 Sn Tin	121.8 51 Sb Antimony	127.6 52 Te Tellurium	126.905 53 I Iodine	131,29 54 Xe Xenon
132.9 55 Cs Caesium	137.3 56 Ba Barium	57-71 +	178.5 72 Hf Hafnium	183.8 73 Ta Tantalum	180.9 74 W Tungsten	186.2 75 Re Rhenium	190.2 76 Os Osmium	192.2 77 Ir Iridium	195.1 78 Pt Platinum	197.0 79 Au Gold	200.6 80 Hg Mercury	204,383 81 Tl Thallium	207.2 82 Pb Lead	209.0 83 Bi Bismuth	[209] 84 Po Polonium	[210] 85 At Astatine	[222] 86 Rn Radon
[223] 87 Fr Francium	226.025 88 Ra Radium	89-103 +	[261] 104 Rf Rutherfordium	[268] 105 Db Dubnium	[271] 106 Sg Seaborgium	[267] 107 Bh Bohrium	[269] 108 Hs Hassium	[276] 109 Mt Meitnerium	[281] 110 Ds Darmstadtium	[281] 111 Rg Roentgenium	[285] 112 Cn Copernicium	[284] 113 Uut Ununtrium	[289] 114 Fl Flerovium	[288] 115 Uup Ununpentium	[293] 116 Lv Livermorium	[294] 117 Uus Ununseptium	[294] 118 Uuo Ununoctium
[316] 119 Uue Ununennium	[320] 120 Ubn Unbinilium																

Lanthanide +	138,906 57 La Lanthanum	140,115 58 Ce Cerium	140,908 59 Pr Praseodymium	144,24 60 Nd Neodymium	144,913 61 Pm Promethium	150,36 62 Sm Samarium	151,965 63 Eu Europium	157,25 64 Gd Gadolinium	158,925 65 Tb Terbium	162,50 66 Dy Dysprosium	164,93 67 Ho Holmium	167,26 68 Er Erbium	168,934 69 Tm Thulium	173,04 70 Yb Ytterbium	174,967 71 Lu Lutetium
Actinide +	227,028 89 Ac Actinium	232,038 90 Th Thorium	231,036 91 Pa Protactinium	238,029 92 U Uranium	237,048 93 Np Neptunium	244,064 94 Pu Plutonium	243,061 95 Am Americium	247,07 96 Cm Curium	247,07 97 Bk Berkelium	251,08 98 Cf Californium	252,083 99 Es Einsteinium	257,095 100 Fm Fermium	258,1 101 Md Mendelevium	259,1 102 No Nobelium	262,11 103 Lr Lawrencium

Alkali metal · Alkaline earth metal · Transition metal · Post-transition metal · Metalloid · Polyatomic nonmetal · Diatomic nonmetal · Noble gas

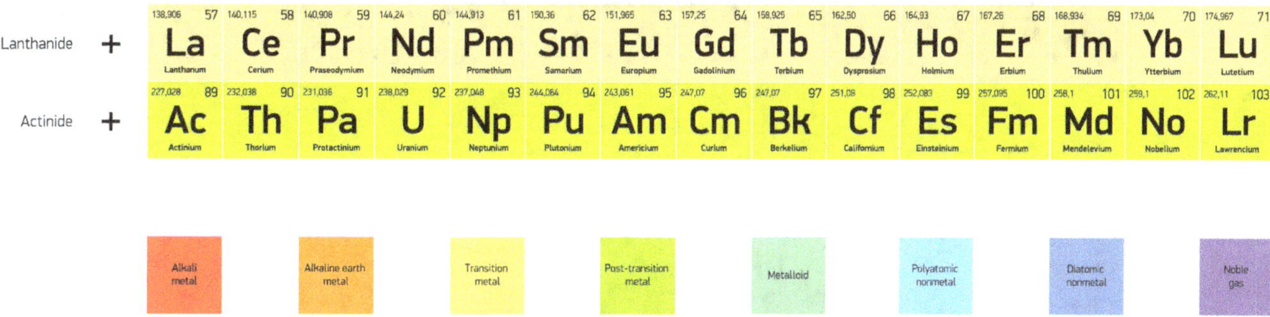

PERIODIC TABLE OF THE ELEMENTS

Legend:
Non-metal · Alkali metal · Alkaline earth metal · Transition metal · Metal · Metalloid · Halogen · Noble gas · Lanthanide · Actinide

1	2												13	14	15	16	17	18
1 H HYDROGEN 1.0079																		**2** He HELIUM 4.0026
3 Li LITHIUM 6.941	**4** Be BERYLLIUM 9.0122												**5** B BORON 10.811	**6** C CARBON 12.011	**7** N NITROGEN 14.007	**8** O OXYGEN 15.999	**9** F FLUORINE 18.998	**10** Ne NEON 20.1797
11 Na SODIUM 22.989	**12** Mg MAGNESIUM 24.305												**13** Al ALUMINIUM 26.981	**14** Si SILICON 28.085	**15** P PHOSPHORUS 30.974	**16** S SULFUR 32.066	**17** Cl CHLORINE 35.453	**18** Ar ARGON 39.948
19 K POTASSIUM 39.098	**20** Ca CALCIUM 40.078	**21** Sc SCANDIUM 44.955	**22** Ti TITANIUM 47.867	**23** V VANADIUM 50.9415	**24** Cr CHROMIUM 51.9961	**25** Mn MANGANESE 54.938	**26** Fe IRON 55.845	**27** Co COBALT 58.933	**28** Ni NICKEL 58.6934	**29** Cu COPPER 63.546	**30** Zn ZINC 65.38		**31** Ga GALLIUM 69.723	**32** Ge GERMANIUM 72.63	**33** As ARSENIC 74.921	**34** Se SELENIUM 78.971	**35** Br BROMINE 79.904	**36** Kr KRYPTON 83.798
37 Rb RUBIDIUM 85.467	**38** Sr STRONTIUM 87.62	**39** Y YTTRIUM 88.9058	**40** Zr ZIRCONIUM 91.224	**41** Nb NIOBIUM 92.9063	**42** Mo MOLYBDENUM 95.95	**43** Tc TECHNETIUM (98)	**44** Ru RUTHENIUM 101.07	**45** Rh RHODIUM 102.90	**46** Pd PALLADIUM 106.42	**47** Ag SILVER 107.8682	**48** Cd CADMIUM 112.414		**49** In INDIUM 114.818	**50** Sn TIN 118.710	**51** Sb ANTIMONY 121.760	**52** Te TELLURIUM 127.60	**53** I IODINE 126.90	**54** Xe XENON 131.293
55 Cs CAESIUM 132.905	**56** Ba BARIUM 137.327	*57-71	**72** Hf HAFNIUM 178.49	**73** Ta TANTALUM 180.94	**74** W TUNGSTEN 183.84	**75** Re RHENIUM 186.207	**76** Os OSMIUM 190.23	**77** Ir IRIDIUM 192.217	**78** Pt PLATINUM 195.084	**79** Au GOLD 196.96	**80** Hg MERCURY 200.59		**81** Tl THALLIUM 204.38	**82** Pb LEAD 207.2	**83** Bi BISMUTH 208.98	**84** Po POLONIUM (209)	**85** At ASTATINE (210)	**86** Rn RADON (222)
87 Fr FRANCIUM (223)	**88** Ra RADIUM (226)	**89-103	**104** Rf RUTHERFORDIUM (267)	**105** Db DUBNIUM (268)	**106** Sg SEABORGIUM (271)	**107** Bh BOHRIUM (272)	**108** Hs HASSIUM (270)	**109** Mt MEITNERIUM (276)	**110** Ds DARMSTADTIUM (281)	**111** Rg ROENTGENIUM (280)	**112** Cn COPERNICIUM (285)		**113** Uut UNUNTRIUM (284)	**114** Fl FLEROVIUM (289)	**115** Uup UNUNPENTIUM (288)	**116** Lv LIVERMORIUM (293)	**117** Uus UNUNSEPTIUM (294)	**118** Uuo UNUNOCTIUM (294)

*** Lanthanides**

57	58	59	60	61	62	63	64	65	66	67	68	69	70	71
La LANTHANUM 138.90	Ce CERIUM 140.116	Pr PRASEODYMIUM 140.90	Nd NEODYMIUM 144.242	Pm PROMETHIUM (145)	Sm SAMARIUM 150.36	Eu EUROPIUM 151.964	Gd GADOLINIUM 157.25	Tb TERBIUM 158.92	Dy DYSPROSIUM 162.500	Ho HOLMIUM 164.93	Er ERBIUM 167.259	Tm THULIUM 168.93	Yb YTTERBIUM 173.054	Lu LUTETIUM 174.9668

**** Actinides**

89	90	90	92	93	94	95	96	97	98	99	100	101	102	103
Ac ACTINIUM (227)	Th THORIUM 232.0377	Pa PROTACTINIUM 231.03	U URANIUM 238.02	Np NEPTUNIUM (237)	Pu PLUTONIUM (244)	Am AMERICIUM (243)	Cm CURIUM (247)	Bk BERKELIUM (247)	Cf CALIFORNIUM (251)	Es EINSTEINIUM (252)	Fm FERMIUM (257)	Md MENDELEVIUM (258)	No NOBELIUM (259)	Lr LAWRENCIUM (262)

The table is divided into groups in order to assist chemists working with these elements to learn and product how an element may behave or react in certain situations.

This table lists the name and abbreviation for each element. You may find some abbreviations easy to remember, such as H which is the abbreviation for hydrogen but some like iron (Fe) and gold (Au) are a somewhat more difficult to remember. In the instance of gold, "Au" originates from "aurum", which is the Latin word for gold.

THE PERIODIC TABLE OF ELEMENTS

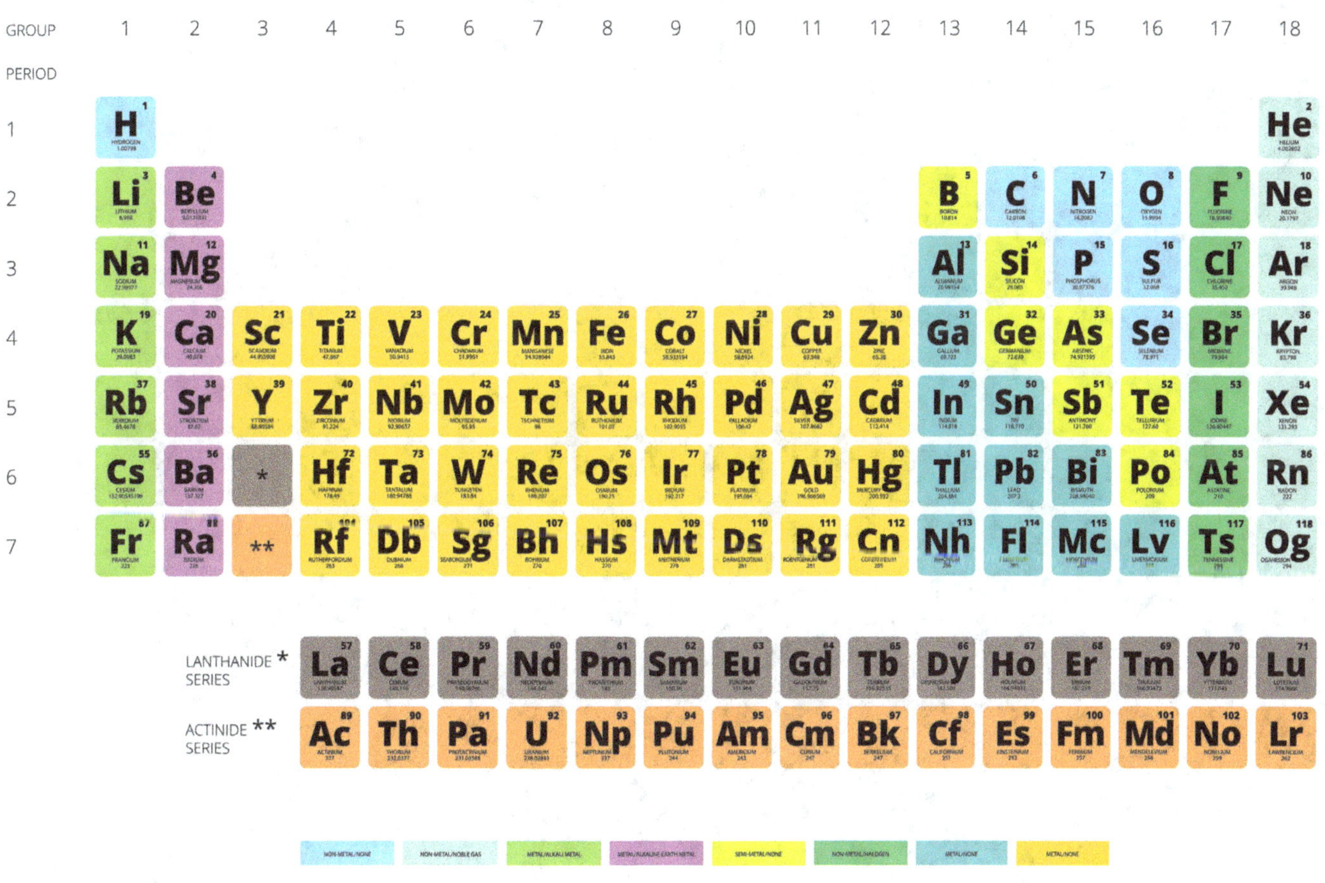

O$_2$

You can learn more by researching on the internet or by reaching out to your teachers, parents, and friends for additional information.

Visit

BABY PROFESSOR
EDUCATION KIDS

www.BabyProfessorBooks.com

to download Free Baby Professor eBooks
and view our catalog of new and exciting
Children's Books